THE COTSWOLDS
Photographs by Bob Croxford

Published by Atmosphere
Willis Vean
Mullion Cornwall TR12 7DF
England
Tel 01326 240180
email info@atmosphere.co.uk

All images Copyright Bob Croxford 2003
All Moral Rights Reserved

ISBN   0 9543409 2 2

Printed and bound in Italy

Cover   SNOWSHILL

CASTLE COMBE is one of the prettiest villages in England

MALMESBURY ABBEY St. Mary's Church PAINSWICK

DUNTISBOURNE LEER

Stone bridge at EASTLEACH MARTIN

The Parish Church at CIRENCESTER

Chipping Steps at TETBURY

The 15th century Market House at TETBURY

Standing stone on MINCHINGHAMPTON COMMON

MINCHINHAMPTON

GLOUCESTER CATHEDRAL   The Beatrix Potter shop in GLOUCESTER

The old canal terminus docks in GLOUCESTER

The Regency Promenade at CHELTENHAM

Caryatids grace Montpellier Parade in CHELTENHAM

GUITING POWER

BROADWAY TOWER

BROADWAY has a wide main street lined with honey coloured shops and houses

The church of St. James and the Jacobean gatehouse at CHIPPING CAMPDEN

Thatched cottage at CHIPPING CAMPDEN

The Market Hall at CHIPPING CAMPDEN was built in 1627

A quiet corner in STANTON

Terraced cottages line the road at BOURTON~ON~THE~HILL.

Thatched cottages at GREAT TEW

The Town Hall at WOODSTOCK

The Redesdale Arms was once a coaching inn at MORETON~IN~MARSH

STOW~ON~THE~WOLD

Picturesque corners in UPPER SLAUGHTER

The Old Mill at LOWER SLAUGHTER

The River Eye at LOWER SLAUGHTER

One of a series of elegant low bridges at BOURTON~ON~THE~WATER

Limestone cottages at ARLINGTON ROW, BIBURY

ARLINGTON ROW

Spring daffodils at SWINBROOK

The Coln River and the Mill at FAIRFORD

Honey coloured streets in BURFORD

Charming corners of FILKINS

The River Thames at LECHLADE

The St. John's Lock on the River Thames at LECHLADE

INDEX

Adelstrop	37
Arlington Row	48, 49, 50
Bourton~on~the~Hill	31
Bourton~on~the~Water	45, 46
Broadway	25
Broadway Tower	24
Burford	56, 57
Castle Coombe	3
Cheltenham	18, 19, 20
Chipping Campden	26, 28, 29
Cirencester	9
Duntisbourne Leer	6
Eastleach Martin	8
Fairford	55
Filkins	58, 59
Gloucester	14, 15, 16
Great Tew	34
Guiting Power	22
Hidcote Bartrim	32
Lechlade	60, 62, 64
Lower Slaughter	42, 44
Malmesbury	4
Minchinghampton	12, 13
Moreton~in~Marsh	36
Northleach	17
Painswick	5
Stanton	30
Stow~in~the~Wold	38, 39
Swinbrook	54
Tetbury	10, 11
Upper Slaughter	40, 41
Winchcombe	21
Windrush	52
Wyke Rissington	53

The church of St. Lawrence and the River Thames at LECHLADE